WHAT YOU SHOULD KNOW

ABOUT THE

SACRAMENTS

◆

CHARLENE ALTEMOSE, MSC

Liguori

ONE LIGUORI DRIVE
LIGUORI MO 63057-9999
314.464.2500

Imprimi Potest:
James Shea, C.SS.R.
Provincial, St. Louis Province
The Redemptorists

Imprimatur:
+ Edward J. O'Donnell, D.D.
Auxiliary Bishop, Archdiocese of St. Louis

ISBN 0-89243-629-8
Library of Congress Catalog Card Number: 94-75243

Copyright © 1994, Charlene Altemose, MSC
Printed in the United States of America
98 99 00 01   6 5 4 3

Interior art by Grady Gunter

CONTENTS

INTRODUCTION

A my and Beth were playing with their dolls on the front porch. "I can't come over tomorrow because I go to Sunday school," said Amy. "Oh, I can't play either," replied Beth. "I'm going to Mass."

"What makes your church different from mine?" asked Amy.

Beth thought a bit. "Well, I'm Catholic and in my Church, God's all over and Jesus comes real over and over and over again." Little Beth has captured the heart of Catholicism and what the sacraments are all about.

To be Catholic is to respect God's presence in all of creation. To be Catholic is to believe that God has shown his love in many ways and most especially by sending his Son, Jesus. To be Catholic is to follow Jesus in the tradition of the apostles and early Christians and to share in Jesus' divine life. To be Catholic is to belong to the community of believers in the Church and to be witness to this belief by an active faith. To be Catholic is to affirm that Jesus "comes real over and over and over again" in the Church, especially through the sacraments.

Catholics are a "God-is-with-us" people, a sacramental people. The seven sacraments—baptism, confirmation, Eucharist, reconciliation, anointing of the sick, holy orders, and matrimony—are a vital part of Catholic identity. Regularly celebrating the sacraments is the earmark of a "practicing Catholic."

The Second Vatican Council considers the sacraments more than ritual moments; they are signs of Christ's abiding presence and encounters with the risen

**PAST,
PRESENT,
FUTURE**

5

Lord. In keeping with that contemporary theology, this booklet explores the sacraments as timeless spiritual realities that link the present, the past, and the future. We celebrate the past, as we remember God's graces to those who have preceded us in faith. We celebrate the present, as we embrace Jesus' sacramental presence with us today. We celebrate the future, as we acknowledge God's expanding grace of help in the future, in this world and the next.

This booklet is divided into four sections. Part I presents a broad overview and explains what it means to be "sacramental" people. This is the essence of our Catholic identity. Parts II, III, and IV explain how each sacrament evolved, is celebrated today, and affects our lives. A basic three-point outline is followed. Through the sacraments we:

a) continue Jesus' mission
b) celebrate Jesus' presence in symbolic ritual
c) connect the sacraments to our life situations

This booklet is limited in scope, but it treats major aspects of sacramental theology and addresses various pastoral concerns regarding revised practices since Vatican II. I hope this booklet promotes a greater knowledge and appreciation of the sacraments and strengthens the faith of those who read it. As young Beth says, "Jesus comes real over and over and over again." We sometimes forget that or take it for granted. This work helps us remember and appreciate.

Part I

CATHOLICS ARE A SACRAMENTAL PEOPLE

The word *sacrament* is as familiar to Catholics as *cookie* is to a toddler. In our growing-up years we learned that "a sacrament is an outward sign instituted by Christ to give grace." This is sacrament in its restricted sense. Broadly speaking, any person, place, or thing that draws us to God or is a sign of God's presence and redemptive love is "sacrament."

The Catholic world view, then, is basically a sacramental view. Catholics consider God as Creator and the whole world as a reflection of God's love. We are a sacramental people, and everything we see points to the Creator, who has saturated the world with divine love.

Jesus: The Sacrament of God

God revealed his creative love most dramatically through Jesus, who has graced the world with his earthly presence. Since then, all creation has been raised to a divine level. Because Jesus reveals the nature of God most perfectly, we say that Jesus is the "sacrament of God."

The Church: The Sacrament of Jesus

Jesus continues his presence through the divine life he shares with us through the Church. The Church, continuing Jesus' presence in the world, can truly be called the "sacrament of Jesus." Catholics share in Jesus' mission by following the tradition of the early Christians and celebrating Christ's presence through the Church and the sacraments.

The Sacraments: Graced Moments in Our Life

The sacraments are special moments and graced spiritual opportunities. The rites of the sacraments take place in individual celebrations and mark a special presence of Jesus with those who approach the sacraments with faith.

When we participate in the sacramental life of the Church, we draw Christ into our human sphere and make his presence part of our human existence. We "Christify" the world and make Christ more visible to our world today.

Through the Sacraments We Continue Christ's Mission

The sacraments did not appear as fully developed celebrations. Rather, the sacraments have developed into what we celebrate today. As each age in Church history has attempted to interpret Christ's promise to be with us always, the sacraments have evolved and still are going through processes of change. This section traces these developments.

Imagine a foreign dignitary's son enrolling in college and not making known his royal origins. You attend classes together, become friends, go to sports events together, join the same fraternity, unaware of his noble roots. At graduation the truth is revealed. How do you react? At first you are amazed, but then you think back on those times when you had a hint of his royalty. In reflective hindsight, his identity becomes clearer, and you come to understand his mysterious ways better.

This is what happened with Jesus. He walked the land and lived simply in Nazareth. He went about doing good and calling for repentance. Some could not accept his virtuous demands. Others hated and derided him and felt threatened by his authority and integrity. Crowds gathered to hear Jesus, but many people came only out of curiosity.

The disciples followed Jesus because they found a certain attractive mystique about him; Jesus made a radical difference in their lives. As Jews, they knew about God, but through Jesus, they came to understand God in a new and different way. Although they were present at miracles and heard Jesus teach, they couldn't quite figure him out. Nevertheless, they followed him with a steadfast faith and commitment.

Jesus lived, suffered, and died to embody God's love present to us in our human condition. The Resurrection affirmed Jesus' divinity. The conviction that "Jesus lives" impelled the disciples to spread the Good News. Jesus lived on in the hearts of believers, in the actions of the gathered assembly, and in the stories remembered and retold in the community. By their very lifestyle, the early Christians were a visible sign of the presence of the risen Lord. They did not *go* to Church; they *were* the Church!

Jesus' disciples continued to use the rituals of the Jewish faith, but these rituals took on a new meaning: they became signs of Jesus' presence. Although we say the sacraments were "instituted by Christ," Jesus did not say to his followers, "I'll be leaving you soon, so here are seven sacraments to continue my work." No! Jesus said "Do this in remembrance of me" (Luke 22:19). So in imitation of Christ's actions, the early Church gathered at the holy meal, accepted new members, healed, forgave, appointed leaders, and practiced and preached love.

As time went on, many came to believe, and the Good News spread. Although their faith in Christ put their lives in jeopardy, Jesus' followers willingly went to their deaths—so strong was their commitment and dedication to him.

By the second century, Christians believed Jesus to be

present in the ritual actions of the gathered assembly and in the sacred Word, the New Testament. Since the early Church was uns1tructured, ritual practices varied according to local customs. The basic faith was the same, however; the early Christians, in celebrating Jesus' life, death, and resurrection, continued his presence and shared in his divine life through actions, signs, and community worship.

The Christian rituals were called *mysterion*, the Greek word that means "mystery." When Latin became the common language in the fourth century, Christians translated *mysterion* as "*sacramentum.*" These sacred signs, sacraments, were ways that Christians believed Jesus continued his presence among them. Blessings, prayers, rituals, anointings, everything holy, were—to them— signs of Christ's presence. At one point, there were as many as forty sacred signs, or sacraments.

In the Middle Ages, as the Church grew more organized, it became necessary to explain and define the rituals. The Second Council of Lyons in 1274 determined which sacred rituals most faithfully mirrored Christ's actions, attitudes, and abiding presence. Seven official signs were named sacraments; other practices and holy signs were called sacramentals.

During the Reformation, baptism and Eucharist were the two sacraments accepted by the Protestant reformers because these were explicitly mentioned in the Bible. The Catholic Church, at the Council of Trent (1545-1563), dogmatically stated that there were seven sacraments, and defined them as "outward signs instituted by Christ to give grace." To safeguard the Church's authentic teaching on the sacraments, the Council emphasized exactness in performing the sacramental rituals. This mind-set, which considered the sacraments as sacred "things," lasted until the Second Vatican Council (1962-1965), when sacramental renewal recaptured the thinking of the early Church: the sacraments are signs of the presence of Christ and encounters with the risen Lord. Jesus is active in the world through the sacraments.

Humans are able to see beneath and beyond what the naked eye perceives. We grasp inner meanings quite naturally. We not only live through experiences but we can make sense out of them. Objects, events, gestures, or words to which we give deeper meanings are symbols that speak loudly and affect us emotionally when words fail.

Through the Sacraments We Celebrate Jesus' Presence in Symbolic Ritual

Symbols can become so familiar, however, that we gradually fail to recognize their significance. In our life of faith, we cannot allow symbols to become rote and meaningless; they need to be a fresh and meaningful part of our lives. This is difficult for us in the late twentieth century. Unlike early civilizations who attributed everything mysterious to their gods, we have a more technologically refined understanding of the universe. We have so many "answers" for what was once naturally unknown. What's more, our "instant" lifestyle lessens our ability to live attuned to the symbolic in our lives.

Thus religion can become rote and lifeless; liturgy and sacramental rites can become endurance tests rather than meaningful experiences. When we revise our ways of thinking, when we ask, "What does it mean?" our sacramental symbolic rituals come alive with significance.

In our sacramental rites we use the common and ordinary: bread, water, wine, oil, gestures, and words. We have invested these with sacred meanings. Our faith enables us to see these everyday things and gestures as signs of Christ's presence. Just as the whole earth was divinized by Jesus, ordinary elements are raised to a new level in sacramental signs and rituals.

When we are attuned to symbolism, we make new discoveries about God, about others, and about ourselves. But understanding symbolism is only part of the full picture. We act out the deeper meanings of our

symbols through ritual. Rituals put motion into our inner feelings. When we wish to mark specific events, we develop rituals. They are as much a part of our being human as is the ability to live symbolically.

Rituals play a significant role in our faith life. They help us delve into the mysteries we celebrate and draw us into the Divine. We easily sense that "the place on which [we] are standing is holy ground" (Exodus 3:5) and revel in the presence of the Sacred. When we take an active part in this divine-human interplay, rituals come alive, renewing us with life and joy.

But how can we pull ourselves into purposeful rituals? How can we become more sensitized to the things of the Spirit? How can we foster greater enthusiasm and overcome boredom? How can we capture the unfolding of divine mysteries when we are so affected by circumstances around us? If our rituals are to be truly meaningful, these are commanding questions.

Wonder: In order to "see with new eyes" and become alive at our sacramental rituals, we need to begin as our Lord recommended: "Unless you change and become like children, you will never enter the kingdom of heaven" (Matthew 18:3).

To be as a little child is to recapture the sense of wonder. Children easily get excited. This newness of life, seeing all things through the eyes of a child, is the launching pad for a spiritual life and a deeper appreciation of the sacraments.

As we mature, our perception about life's mysteries becomes jaded, but our sense of wonder can be recaptured through faith and reflection. As the fox told the Little Prince, "It's only with the heart that we can see rightly; what is essential is invisible to the eye." We need to see the relationship between the world and the spirit. Wonder gives birth to faith, and faith breeds a sense of God. If we can be gripped at the sight of a frizzy dandelion or a colorful sunset, then it's possible to experience Christ in the sacraments. The words, gestures, and objects beckon to us: "God is here. Come to meet him."

Peace be with you

Words: Words are an intimate form of communication and are essential components of rituals. When we share words with others, we give them part of our inner being. Words bond us intimately to other persons. Words possess an inherent magic, for they can bring about any desired effect; they can lift sagging spirits, bolster enthusiasm, hurt deeply, and turn indifference into love.

When God broke into history and developed a relationship with the human family, he chose the medium of the word to convey his message of love. God realized the dynamism inherent in the human word. These human words of the sacred writers are called the "word of God"; they reveal God to us. This sharing of God's life through the human experiences of the people of Israel and the early Christians are for us the prototype of how God continues to break into history and reveal his love. That's why the Scriptures are such a vital element in our faith.

For us Christians, the Hebrew Scriptures (Old Testament) and the Christian Scriptures (New Testament) comprise the Word of God. The history of the Jewish people prepares the way for God's ultimate gift of love, his Son, Jesus Christ, whose life and teachings are recorded in the New Testament.

Through God's Word, sacred Scripture, we can grasp the deeper meanings of our Catholic rituals. Each sacramental rite retells the story of God's love as recorded in the Bible. How intimately connected with our sacramental rituals is God's word!

When a passage of Scripture is read during sacramental celebrations, the words become more meaningful when we ask ourselves, *What is this passage saying to me now? How does this passage help me see God's continuing actions?* So that the sacraments can speak more directly to individual situations, options for Scripture passages are allowed and provided in the revised sacramental rituals.

The divine themes of God's love, compassion, forgiveness, and freedom, as set forth in Scripture, are aptly portrayed in the sacramental rites. To live sacramentally, Catholics need to become familiar with the Bible and attuned to biblical themes. When we link the scriptural story with our sacramental rituals and symbols, God's presence is more easily defined.

Celebration: We not only act out our feelings but we observe and remember certain events. We set time apart to absorb their significance by entering into celebrations. We escape the humdrum daily routine and put new vigor into living by celebrating.

The dictionary defines celebration as honor and praise in a public display. In moments of celebration, we publicly acclaim someone for an accomplishment or a milestone; we link the past, the present, and the future of a memorable experience in a single ritual, as at a graduation.

Celebrations are convenient outlets for experiences we wish to remember. Tales told and retold become memories of gatherings and festivities. Sometimes we celebrate spontaneously, but the more memorable the event, the more detailed and elaborate will be the preparations and planning. Think of what it takes to arrange a wedding!

The visible signs of the seven sacraments are a public affirmation and celebration of our life in Christ. We are not an indiscriminate conglomeration, but believers bound in a common faith. The Church today "celebrates" the sacraments, publicly acclaiming the presence of Jesus in our midst. We do not passively "receive" the sacraments; we actively celebrate the presence of Christ with us.

The renewed rites emphasize the social aspects of the sacraments as community celebrations. We express in a group what our faith means to us personally and join with the prayers of the entire Church. The sacraments, the Church's official worship, ideally take place at a eucharistic liturgy or within a community gathered in faith.

Rituals need to be the possession of the whole group. There are no spectators in the revised rituals; all are active participants, though with differing roles: those who celebrate the sacrament and those who participate in that celebration. For a sacramental celebration to be effective, each person's role must be clearly defined and the symbols and language used must be fully grasped. Otherwise, the ritual will be rote and lifeless.

Through the Sacraments We Connect Our Faith to Our Daily Lives

The sacraments not only recall the past and bring Christ's redemptive graces into the present; the sacraments extend their effects into our days and into eternity. We call this extension of the sacraments in time sacramentality. The following anecdote illustrates this point.

A seasoned trucker was traveling with a rookie on a cross-country trip. "Why do you seem so fresh? You don't look at all tired and bored," the lad remarked after a long day. The veteran replied, "Well, son, for you this was a workday, but for me, I look at it as a lovely ride in the countryside. I get as much out of it as I can and enjoy the sights along the way."

When the sacraments are considered as the "Catholic thing to do" or a religious "duty," when we are concerned more with externals and requirements, we're like the rookie driver. We only go through the motions and miss the deeper experience. But when we regard the sacraments as the seasoned trucker considered his work, we "experience more." We recognize the presence of the Lord more fully when we apply the fruits of the sacra-

ments to our daily routines and lifestyles. The sacraments, as celebrations of the Lord's presence, color and flavor our entire life.

The early Christians never spoke of "receiving sacraments." They believed that in celebrating Eucharist and performing the holy actions, they were meeting the resurrected Christ and were extending his presence into the world by their witness. We need to recapture this attitude. As members of the Church we share Jesus' life through the sacraments and in turn, we are called to share the life of Jesus with others and spread it throughout the world.

This "sacramental domino effect" is more clearly seen in the image of a wheel. Jesus is the hub and center of our spiritual life. Through his redemption, it is possible for us to link with God most intimately. The sacraments are the spokes of the wheel. We, the Church, form the outer rim, bound together in Christ and function as a unified body. We tap into the spiritual reserves of the hub when we make use of the sacraments.

The wheel, however, is of no value by itself. To be of any use, it must move. So also the spiritual energy of the sacraments needs to be put into action in our lives. That's sacramentality!

Sacramentality may be a new word in our Catholic vocabulary, but it is not a recent theological discovery; it's as old as Christianity. In the simplest definition, sacramentality is the practical application of the sacraments to our daily lives. Authentic Catholic sacramental life does not end with rituals but is a beginning for celebrating God's love and presence in one's life. Sacramentality is "grace after the ritual," daily life "sacramentalized."

Part II

The Sacraments of Belonging:
BAPTISM, CONFIRMATION, AND EUCHARIST

We enter this world belonging to an age, a culture, a native land, and a family. Belonging is part of our natural heritage. In addition to the genetic and personality traits we inherit from our parents, we are influenced by their faith, attitudes, values, and notions about God as well. As we mature, we depend on others to provide us with meaning and security. We grow into larger social circles that furnish us with a sense of belonging and enable us to develop into useful members of society.

Belonging to a group that shares a common faith supports us in our spiritual life. Catholics have this unity in belief in the Church and the sacraments. Whether one is Catholic at birth or by choice later in life, the Church incorporates new members through the sacraments of initiation: baptism, confirmation, and Eucharist.

BAPTISM

Our family provides our natural sustenance, but we come into this world without a specific spiritual identity. Baptism provides us with a faith identity, welcomes us into a community of believers, and incorporates us into the family of Jesus.

Baptism Continues Jesus' Mission

From the beginning of time persons have been initiated into groups through purifications and baptisms. For the Jewish people, these rites were part of their religious practices. In the New Testament, Jesus is baptized by John. Thus, Jesus affirmed his mission and showed a complete solidarity with our humanity. Although we have no record that the early followers of Jesus were baptized, we do know that Jesus commissioned the apostles to baptize in the name of the Father, the Son, and the Holy Spirit.

Baptism, as we know it, has undergone many changes in its history. In the early Church, one who wished to become a Christian pledged faith in Jesus and was baptized. When Christianity became the official religion of the Roman Empire (A.D. 380), the Church required a preparation period, the catechumenate, for those who wished to become Christian. This was a period of instruction in the Christian way of life and an opportunity for the person to verify his or her absolute sincerity. Because baptism signified a dying with Jesus, persons stepped into a pool and were submerged into the water. To signify a rising with Christ, they ascended three steps and were clothed in white garments. As the Church grew, a simpler method of initiation was practiced and infant baptism became the norm.

Saint Augustine preached baptism as being necessary for salvation to cleanse us from the evil tendency which he labeled original sin. Another breakthrough in baptismal theology occurred in the Middle Ages. The question arose concerning unbaptized, virtuous persons who lived before Christ. Saint Thomas Aquinas taught that there is a baptism of desire for those who through no fault of their own were not baptized, and a baptism of blood for those who gave up their life for Christ before they were baptized.

Medieval theologians provided an acceptable solution to the question of infants who die without baptism:

they enter "Limbo," a state of natural happiness. This was comforting, but never has been a doctrine of faith.

The Council of Trent affirmed the necessity of baptism. Because human beings are born into original sin, infants were to be baptized as soon as possible. This custom lasted until the renewal of the Second Vatican Council, which sought new directions in baptismal practices and rituals. In light of that renewal, baptism is seen primarily as a commitment to Christ, not only a cleansing which erases original sin.

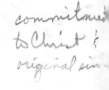

Baptism After Vatican II: One of the most dramatic changes of Vatican II concerned the admission of adults into the Church. The catechumenate, the Rite of Christian Initiation of Adults (RCIA), was reinstated as the norm for adults to come into the Church.

Infant baptism, too, underwent a shift of emphasis. Today we are not as much concerned with the effect of baptism on the infant's soul as we are with the parents' practice of their faith. What good is it if an infant is baptized and grows up without the warmth and support of a caring faith community? Today, the evangelization of the parents is a major baptismal emphasis.

Baptism Celebrates the Presence of Jesus in Symbolic Ritual

Water, the necessary element at baptism, effects in a spiritual sense what water signifies in the physical world: newness of life, growth, cleansing, death, and resurrection. Chrism, a mixture of olive oil and balm used in biblical days, denotes dedication. At baptism, the chrism signifies our share in Christ's royal priesthood and divine life. The individual baptismal candle, lit from the paschal candle, reminds the baptized to carry the light of Christ into the world. White garments symbolize the innocence and purity of the newly baptized.

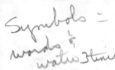

The Symbols and Rite of Baptism: One is baptized by being immersed in the baptismal water or by having water poured over one's head, while the words of baptism are said: "N., I baptize you in the name of the Father,/ and of the Son,/ and of the Holy Spirit." This threefold immersion or pouring water over the head and the words are the bare essentials of the baptismal rite. In an emergency, water is poured on the forehead while the words are said. If there is doubt whether a person has been baptized or it cannot be proved to be valid, one is baptized conditionally, beginning with the words, "If you are not already baptized" (Canon #869).

The solemn celebration of baptism takes place at the baptistry, a simple font or separate section in church. Baptism by immersion is becoming more commonly used because this manner more clearly emphasizes "dying and rising with Christ." Some churches have installed a baptismal pool.

In an emergency, anyone may baptize, but the ordinary minister of solemn baptism is a bishop, priest, or deacon. Since baptism marks us as a Christian for life and enables us to celebrate the other sacraments, it can be celebrated only once and the event must be carefully noted in the official parish registry.

Baptismal Sponsors: At least one godparent is required at baptism. Since the early days of the Church, sponsors have been part of the Church's tradition to attest to the sincerity of those coming into the Church. In the Middle Ages, life spans were shorter and the probability of a child losing his or her parents was common, so godparents often became surrogate parents. Today, a sponsor's role is basically a spiritual relationship, a representative of the community and, in the case of infants, a support to the parents. Adults who are to be baptized also have a sponsor who acts as a spiritual guide and a baptismal witness.

To be a sponsor or godparent, one must be a practicing Catholic at least sixteen years old. A baptized Christian of another denomination may be a witness at baptism provided there is a Catholic sponsor.

Infant Baptism: Formerly infant baptisms were private, usually performed with only godparents and family attending. Today the sacraments are seen as community celebrations and so ideally baptism of infants takes place during a special baptism liturgy.

Parents play a key role in the ritual for baptism of infants and children who have not yet reached the age of reason. Prior to baptism, the parents and godparents are prepared and instructed. The ritual prayers stress their responsibility for the faith formation of the children.

As the parents and godparents present the child, they are asked about their expectations of the Church and what they have named the child. The child's name is significant because it gives identity to the child and is the name by which the child will be known. Traditionally it was to be a saint's name, but the *Code of Canon Law* states that "a Christian name in the sense of a saint's name is not required but only one that is not alien or offensive to Christian sensibilities" (#855). Parents and godparents promise solemnly to raise the child in the Catholic faith and verify this as they trace the sign of the cross on the child's forehead. The parents are in effect saying, "I appreciate the faith as a stronghold in my life, and I wish to pass this heritage on to my child." This signing with the cross is a powerful symbolic gesture and should be done with conscious awareness.

The baptismal water is blessed and the parents and godparents publicly renew their own baptismal vows and affirm their own faith. To ward off evil influences, a prayer for exorcism is said and the child is anointed before and after baptism as a sign of spiritual strength and commitment to Christ. Then the rite of baptism takes place.

To symbolize the cleansing of sin and one's closeness to God in baptism, a white garment is placed on the newly baptized. The priest then touches the ears and mouth of the one baptized and prays for openness to the Word of God. A candle is then lit from the paschal candle and handed to the parent or godparent while the priest prays that the light of Christ will illumine one's life. Prayers of blessing for the mother, the father, and those gathered conclude the ceremony.

Adult Baptism: The Rite of Christian Initiation of Adults is the norm for adults to become full members of the Catholic Church. The theme of community dominates the RCIA process because Catholicism is community-oriented. Those interested in the Catholic faith usually sign up at a parish and begin the RCIA process guided by an RCIA team.

The RCIA process is divided into four phases, marked at specific times with symbolic rites celebrated in the presence of the community. The precatechumenate is the period of inquiry and clarification. One's questions about the faith are answered and faith stories are shared. At the end of this period, the Rite of Entrance into the Catechumenate is celebrated. The candidate becomes a catechuman, the second RCIA phase.

The catechumens are instructed and participate in the Liturgy of the Word at Sunday Mass. To become more acquainted with the liturgical Scriptures, the catechumens leave the church after the homily to "break open the word." Through discussion, reflection, and prayer, the catechumens decide if they wish to continue the process.

THE ELECT

The catechumenate is completed on the first Sunday of Lent by the Rite of Election at which one officially requests to become a full-fledged Catholic. The catechumens then become known as the elect. To signify one's acceptance by the community, the person's name is entered into the Book of the Elect. This ceremony often takes place in the cathedral of the diocese in the presence of the bishop.

Lent, the period of purification and enlightenment, is a special time of conversion for the elect as it is for the whole community. In fact, the tradition of Lent as forty days of penance and conversion began with the catechumens in the early Church. Scrutinies, or prayers for healing and deliverance from evil, held on three successive Sundays in Lent, serve as a reminder of everyone's need for conversion.

For the elect, Holy Saturday is a day of reflection and prayer. The elect usually gather earlier in the day for preparatory rites. They recite the Nicene Creed, after which is the rite of Ephphetha, or opening of the ears. Their Christian name is given and they are anointed with the oil of catechumens. If one has already been baptized in another Christian denomination, this is an opportunity to celebrate the sacrament of reconciliation.

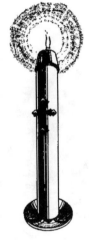

The Easter Vigil celebration is the high point in one's entrance into the Church. The ceremony dramatically portrays the full richness of the Church's symbolism. Light and life are the dominant themes celebrated in pomp and splendor. The Easter water is solemnly blessed and the elect are baptized, confirmed, and participate fully at the Eucharist. Those who have already been baptized celebrate confirmation and Eucharist. The elect are then full-fledged members of the Church and are welcomed by the Catholic community.

To allow the new Catholic, called a neophyte, to explore the truths of faith more deeply and to reflect on the experience, a further period of formation, *mystagogia* (the Greek word for mystery), continues until Pentecost. The new Catholic learns more about the faith and is invited to share fully in the life and ministry of the parish.

Since the RCIA is a recent innovation, parishes may find difficulty in getting it off the ground. A few dedicated Catholics willing to invest their time and share their faith are the catalysts of beginning. The RCIA process is not carved in stone and allows for adaptations and flexibility.

Baptism Connects Our Faith to Our Life Situations

Baptism is not the end of the road but the beginning of a personal journey of faith, as the baptized are bonded to the person and teachings of Jesus through the Church. Once we are baptized, our lives are Christ focused and all we do mirrors Christ, whom we represent in this world.

Baptism and the Individual: For "cradle Catholics" the rite of baptism centers on the parents rather than on the infant. When parents request the baptism of their child, they are expected to cherish and practice their faith, and understand the serious responsibility they are assuming. After all, parents and the family are the primary church the young child will experience. The child will grow to love and appreciate the Church in proportion to the way the parents love and appreciate the Catholic faith. For that reason, an infant's baptism may be delayed until the parents become active in their faith.

Vatican II specifically states that parents are the primary educators of their children, especially regarding religious formation. Although Catholic school or parish religious education programs provide formal instructions in the faith, they are of little use if the religious instruction is contradicted by the parents' negative attitude and lack of religion in the home.

Baptism, too, takes away original sin. We believe that the evil in the world affects our relationship with God. Theologians today explain original sin as a societal reality that affects us all very personally rather than a personal indictment.

Being born into original sin is like a fish in polluted waters. To survive, the fish must be taken out of that environment and put into fresh water. Similarly, we are born into a milieu of evil and sin. In baptism we are introduced into a community of faith, grace, and new life.

Some people still question the fate of unbaptized infants who die. Belief in Limbo consoles, but it is a traditional concept, not a doctrine of faith. Due to our limited understanding of God's ways, we rely on divine mercy and compassion.

When adults enter into full communion with the Catholic Church, they make a free choice, often the result of much prayer and discernment. Even though one has been baptized in another Christian denomination, the decision to become a Catholic may involve a conversion to the Catholic way of life and a radical acceptance of the teachings of the Church. Adults who become Catholic often become very fervent in the practice of their faith due to serious reflection, soul searching, and an effective RCIA experience.

Those who enter the Church as adults are freed of original sin, as well as all personal sin. The Church teaches that those who die after baptism are forgiven all personal sins, as well as the punishment due them, and are admitted directly into heaven. That's why in the early Church, when personal sin could be forgiven only once, baptism was deferred until one was near death.

Baptism and the Church Community: Baptism not only changes an individual but it affects the entire faith community. The Church grows and the presence of Christ is intensified in the world by the commitment and witness of the baptized. When the RCIA is alive, when parents are involved in the religious education of their children, when parishioners take an active interest in the parish, the true Christian spirit is more diffused into the world.

Pastoral Concerns: Because baptism is operative at the local level of a parish, it is vital for Catholics to identify and actively participate in the life of a specific parish. Just as it's important that medical and dental records be on file, so also it's vital that one identifies with a parish that keeps one's sacramental records.

Active Catholics need to reach out to those who have been baptized Catholic and have not been practicing their faith. All they may need is a caring invitation to join in worship and be welcomed warmly into a parish community of faith.

CONFIRMATION

The Holy Spirit has always been central to Catholic belief. The dogma of the Trinity puts into words the relationship of the Father, Son, and Spirit. The theology of the sacrament of confirmation affirms this teaching.

Initially, confirmation was part of one's Christian initiation into the faith. It also was recognized as the fulfillment of Jesus' promise to send the Paraclete, the Holy Spirit. Today, confirmation is celebrated as the sacrament of the Holy Spirit, the completion of baptism, and a Christian's witness to a mature faith. Each of these labels defines the sacrament from different theological viewpoints.

Confirmation Continues Jesus' Mission

From early times persons have been affirmed in their role by rituals of anointings, commissioning them to be bold witnesses to what they believed. In the Hebrew Scriptures, prophets, kings, and others were anointed in their tasks of governing and proclaiming. The Spirit of the Lord figured prominently in Jewish theology and Scripture.

In the New Testament, Jesus promised that when he would no longer be with the disciples, the Paraclete, the Spirit of truth, would come to teach them. (See John 16:13.) Then, on Pentecost, amid wind and fire, the Spirit descended upon those gathered in the Upper Room. This marked the day on which the Church was publicly revealed and spread to other peoples. The Acts of the Apostles records how new followers of "the way" were received as Christians.

For several hundred years in the early Church, one became a full-fledged Christian in a single initiation presided over by the bishop. One was baptized, anointed, shared in the Lord's Supper, and was commissioned by the laying on of hands.

Over the years as the Church spread, the presbyters (priests) were allowed to baptize, and then the baptized reaffirmed their Christian commitment to the bishop during his occasional visits. On those visits, the bishop "confirmed" the baptized, anointing them and laying his hands on them as a sign of their baptismal commitment. As this "confirmation" by the bishop became a widespread practice, confirmation developed into a separate ritual. In 1274, the Second Council of Lyons officially recognized confirmation as one of the seven sacraments.

During the Middle Ages, confirmation guarded one against the evils counteracting the Church. The full-fledged Christian, as a "soldier of Christ," was given a slight blow on the cheek after being anointed. This practice continued until Vatican II.

The Council of Trent (1545-1563) reinforced confirmation as a defense of the faith and decreed that those who are baptized be confirmed. When Pope Pius X decreed that communion be received at an early age, the sequence of the sacraments' reception shifted. Confirmation was placed after penance and Communion. This sequence is still in practice today.

Confirmation After Vatican II: Vatican II linked confirmation to baptism as the second sacrament of initiation. As a result, different theological explanations concerning the nature and purpose of confirmation have been developed. Practical ways to implement this renewed understanding by meaningful catechesis and ritual celebration are still being explored and debated.

Confirmation Celebrates the Presence of Jesus in Symbolic Ritual

One who is baptized and is able to affirm one's baptismal vows can celebrate confirmation. Canon law states that all the baptized are capable of celebrating confirmation (#889).

Preparation for confirmation for those baptized as infants has been a part of formal religious education, usually after celebrating the sacraments of penance and first Communion. In the past, confirmation preparation stressed an intellectual grasp of the faith. Today, confirmation is understood as a sacrament of Christian witness and concern as well. Together with a knowledge of the faith, preparation for confirmation includes service projects so the confirmands are more aware of the social dimension of Christian responsibility.

For adults, the RCIA process provides the ideal preparation for confirmation, which is conferred at the Easter Vigil or on Pentecost.

The Symbols and Rite of Confirmation: Oil has always signified strength and courage; it has been used since ancient times to confirm people in their appointed and accepted missions. The chrism used to anoint is a mixture of oil and balm, solemnly blessed by the bishop at a special Holy Thursday liturgy, along with all the oils used in baptism, confirmation, holy orders, and anointing of the sick.

At confirmation, a sponsor serves the same purpose as

the baptismal sponsor: to be a support to one's faith. It's recommended that the same person serve as sponsor for both baptism and confirmation.

As the confirmand is being anointed, the sponsor stands behind the confirmand and places his or her right hand on the confirmand's right shoulder. The confirmand is called by name, either the baptismal name or one chosen as the confirmation name.

Confirmation takes place in the parish in the presence of the assembly, which symbolizes the presence of the kingdom of God on earth. The whole community is enriched by the gifts of the Spirit.

The bishop is the original minister of confirmation, but a priest may be authorized to confirm. The bishop's presence serves as a symbol of the link of the local church to the Church universal.

To show its connection with the other sacraments of initiation, confirmation usually takes place at a eucharistic liturgy during which the confirmands renew their baptismal vows.

The rite itself is simple. After a prayer to invoke the Holy Spirit, the bishop and priests extend their hands over those to be confirmed. The solemn prayer to the Holy Spirit signifies commission by the Church to witness to the faith.

The bishop anoints each confirmand on the forehead with chrism while saying, "N., be sealed with the Gift of the Holy Spirit." The bishop then extends the sign of peace to the confirmand.

During the Easter Vigil, confirmation takes place immediately following the baptismal rite.

The rite of confirmation is filled with references to the role of the Holy Spirit in one's life. The Scripture readings and prayers call on the aid of the Holy Spirit.

Confirmation Connects Our Faith to Our Life Situations

The rite of confirmation is an empty ritual if the celebration does not prod one to respond to the challenges of the sacrament by a virtuous active Christian life.

The grace of confirmation is kept alive by bringing Christ's goodness into the world through the power of the Holy Spirit. Therefore, one should strive to learn more about the Church and issues which affect the world and one's life. Being active in one's parish, enrolling in adult education classes and Bible study, attending retreats, joining the RCIA team to inform new Catholics, and reaching out to the needy are all practical ways one can live out the confirmation commitment.

Confirmation and the Individual: Confirmation enables us to live out our commitment with the seven gifts of the Holy Spirit, listed by Isaiah 11:2-3: wisdom, understanding, knowledge, counsel, fortitude, piety, and wonder in God's presence (also called fear of the Lord).

When God is a part of our daily living, our lives reflect a spiritual dimension and the effects of the Holy Spirit are evident. Saint Paul lists those traits which signify a truly Godlike life (Galatians 5:22-23). These traditionally have been named the twelve fruits of the Holy Spirit: love, joy, peace, patience, kindness, generosity, tolerance, gentleness, faithfulness, modesty, continence, and chastity.

At our confirmation, each of us publicly affirms our willingness to let God be a part of our life and that the life of Christ will be our model. We know this is no human endeavor, but a grace and gift of God. It's the Holy Spirit who inspires us when our baser selves are stubborn; it's the Holy Spirit who implants in us the desire to do good; it's the grace of the Holy Spirit that enables us to carry on when all seems so useless and hopeless.

Confirmation and the Church Community: Each confirmation celebration witnesses to the presence of the Holy Spirit within the Church. Although it might not be amid wind and fire, still the Spirit is alive in parishes where a vibrant faith is exercised. The more intensely the Spirit's presence is shown, the more the Church will be a credible sign of Christ in the world.

The charismatic movement has done much to heighten our awareness of the role of the Holy Spirit in our lives. However, "baptism of the Spirit" and charismatic prayer are expressions of a special spirituality to which not everyone feels inclined.

The sacrament of confirmation is the Church's official sacramental celebration of the Spirit to which every baptized person is called.

Pastoral Concerns: Canon law states that the age of confirmation is the age of discretion or the age stipulated by the conference of bishops. Because confirmation has been considered a sacrament of maturity, it is usually celebrated in early or later teens. This practice is debated, and the age varies from diocese to diocese.

Confirmation traditionally has concluded one's formal religious education. This trend has spawned the idea that one needs no further formation. Just as commencement marks one's entry into real life, so confirmation marks the beginning of one's deeper involvement with one's faith.

But Catholics need ongoing formation to be conversant in issues of the Church today. Where the Holy Spirit is alive, parishes provide meaningful liturgies, activities, and enrichment programs for every age and interest group, and outreach to the needy. Ideal parishes are those in which the love of God is manifested and the persons radiate this in joy and dedication.

Jesus chose to remain sacramentally present to each age through universal staples of food and drink: bread and wine. Eucharist, the body and blood of Jesus under the appearances of bread and wine, is the heart of Catholic belief and worship. Eucharist, the third sacrament of initiation, completes one's baptism and confirmation commitment. Although there are many dimensions to Eucharist, this work considers Eucharist as sacramental Communion.

Eucharist Continues Jesus' Mission

Jesus solemnly celebrated the Jews' release from bondage in Egypt at the Passover each year. Knowing that his death was near, Jesus wished to remain with his followers in a special way. He chose the community meal.

At the Passover meal on the eve of his death, Jesus took bread and wine and said, "Take and eat, for this is my body. Take and drink. This is my blood."

To remember Jesus after he left this earth, the disciples gathered to "do this in remembrance." Because they believed that Jesus was present through bread and wine in a special way, the meal came to be known as the Lord's supper. The early Church was formed around this "table of the Lord." When Jesus' followers no longer went to the synagogue for prayer, the meal became their wor-ship service and was called "Eucharist": in thanksgiving.

After Christianity was named the official religion of the Roman Empire in A.D. 380, Christian worship was celebrated in public, and the liturgy became ceremonial and ritualistic. As Christianity spread, each village built its own church and varying local customs determined the eucharistic liturgy. The faithful brought food as gifts and partook of the body and blood of Christ under the appearances of bread and wine. Communion in the early Church was part of the meal, shared by fully initiated Christians.

At the Council of Lyons in 1274, Eucharist was named one of the seven sacraments. The Eucharistic sacrifice was seen as the unbloody sacrifice of the Cross making present Jesus' death on Calvary, thus enabling the faithful to share in the redemptive merits of Jesus' death.

The laity felt themselves unworthy of the body and blood of Christ, so they rarely received Communion. Eventually, a Church law, still in effect today, decreed that Communion be received at least once during Eastertime (First Sunday of Lent until Trinity Sunday).

Since there were fewer communions, unleavened wafers replaced loaves of bread. These were called hosts from the Latin word *hostia* which means "victim"; Jesus was the victim in the unbloody sacrifice of the Cross. To avoid spoilage or spilling of wine, Communion was given under the appearance of bread alone. The Council of Trent reaffirmed eucharistic doctrine and the requirements for Communion, but the Jansenist movement of the seventeenth century, which preached human sinfulness and unworthiness, contributed to the continuing practice of infrequent Communion.

In 1910, Pope Pius X decreed that Communion should be received frequently and be given to children. This changed the order and ages at which the sacraments were celebrated. In 1964 the eucharistic fast was reduced to one hour before Communion.

Eucharist After Vatican II: Vatican II expressed the theological richness of the Eucharist by noting its various aspects: the Lord's supper, sacred banquet, breaking of the bread, holy sacrifice, memorial of Christ's passion, death and resurrection, sacred liturgy, and paschal mystery. The Eucharist is the summit of worship and the fountain from which all spiritual graces flow.

The laity is encouraged to fuller participation in Eucharist by celebrating Communion each time they attend Mass. Commissioned by the bishop as eucharistic ministers, laypeople may bring Communion to the sick and distribute Communion at Mass when there is a large number of communicants.

Eucharist Celebrates the Presence of Jesus in Symbolic Ritual

Jesus chose the most common and familiar elements of daily life as the form in which he is present to us throughout the ages: bread and wine. The rite that surrounds Eucharist is deeply rooted in both Scripture and tradition.

The Symbols and Rite of Communion: Bread, as a universal staple, and wine, as a common drink, perfectly symbolize Jesus as our nourishment and spiritual strength.

The small hosts the faithful receive are flattened unleavened wafers baked on special appliances similar to waffle irons engraved with liturgical symbols. The host that the priest uses is larger, about three inches in diameter, so it can be easily seen when it is elevated during Mass.

The wine used at Mass is made from grapes and may be Communion for the faithful on special occasions. During Mass, a drop of water is added to the wine to signify Jesus' humanity.

As the priest says the words of consecration during Mass, the bread and wine are changed into the body and blood of Christ. This is called "transubstantiation."

Any baptized Catholic who is free from serious sin and who can believe the host as the body of Christ may receive Communion. Out of respect for the sacredness of the sacrament, one refrains from solid food and drink, excluding water and medicine, one hour before Communion. The aged, sick, and those who care for them are exempt from the eucharistic fast.

Persons ordinarily celebrate Eucharist at Mass. Communion can be given outside of Mass, however; it can be brought to the sick at any time. Communion, available daily, can be received twice on the same day only during Mass or (as Viaticum) in danger of death (Canon #917).

Ordinarily, Communion is given under the appearance of bread. To show more clearly the full sign of Eucharist, Vatican II allows Communion under both species of bread and wine.

The communicant has the option to take Communion on the tongue or in the hand. Communion in the hand was introduced to more clearly signify Jesus' directive to "take and eat." Receiving Communion with an open outstretched hand in the stance of a beggar helps us remember our poverty and dependence upon the Lord.

The communicant stands before the eucharistic minister who shows the host and says, "Body of Christ," to which the communicant responds "Amen," as a devout and conscious affirmation of faith.

Eucharist Connects Our Faith to Our Life Situations

Eucharist is not primarily an action, a "receiving" of our Lord. Rather, Eucharist is a way of living, a continuous thanksgiving, an active participation in the mission of Christ.

Eucharist and the Individual: By our baptism, we are all called to "be Eucharist." As we receive Christ into our very being, Christ literally dwells in us, and we are called to show forth that presence in the world. Thus, we cannot look at Eucharist as merely an obligation or a personal form of piety. Vatican II challenges us to realize the social implications of Eucharist: Christ comes to us so we may be Christ and Eucharist for others.

Eucharist is active. We are forgiven so we may forgive. We receive so that we may give. We come together so we may go forth and bring Christ to the world. We affirm our unity with Christ so we can be Christ for others. We

35

are fed with spiritual food so we may nourish the world with our grace and goodness.

Christ comes to us as bread. If bread is left to stand, it becomes stale and useless. The bread of Eucharist that we consume must be activated to satisfy the hungers around us. We must strive to make our niche in the world a more eucharistic place—that is, Christ becoming present in the human situation.

We cannot truly find Christ if we ignore the cries of those less fortunate. Christ's presence in Eucharist is God's special gift to us; Christ's presence in us is our gift to the world. To "be Eucharist" is to incorporate into our own personal being all that Christ is and expects of us. "Be you perfect as I intend you to be" is our challenge as we receive the Lord in Communion.

The Incarnation bridged the gap between heaven and earth. Eucharist, too, joins the material world with the sacred. We cannot "live church" on Sunday and forget it on Monday. We bring a sacred dimension into the world when Eucharist is part of every facet of our life.

We all need the Lord's constant help in our life. Communion serves as our spiritual nourishment, for we hunger for wholeness and meaning. We wish to be as perfect as God has intended, but something in our inner being pulls us away and weans us from the good. This proneness to be somehow less than we can be causes us to make poor choices because we are not focused on the Lord.

Eucharist is strength for this weakness, a focus and center for our fragmented selves. We come to Eucharist less than perfect and go away a better person. When we approach the Lord's table with a heart of love, our sins are forgiven and forgotten. Eucharist is the road of beginning again.

Eucharist and the Church Community: The expanded understanding of our faith through Vatican II makes us more aware of the social dimension of Eucharist. It was in the community, gathered at a most solemn meal, that the Lord gave us himself. At the gathering in the liturgy, the Lord again comes to us. From its inception, Eucharist has always been a community happening. This is often beautifully evident when parishes celebrate first holy Communion; it's a very special day for the entire faith community.

Although Christ comes to us as individuals, the full stature of the Body of Christ is shown most powerfully in a vibrant community of believers. The more the liturgy and Eucharist show forth our solidarity and concern for others, the more effective will be our personal Communion. Eucharist necessarily goes beyond the ambience of the church walls. Eucharist of the altar becomes Eucharist to the world as the worshipers scatter after Mass.

Pastoral Concerns: Eucharist celebrates complete membership in the Catholic Church and is a sign of perfect unity in faith. Communion in Catholic churches may be celebrated only by those who fully share the Catholic faith of Eastern or Western rites. Roman Catholics may celebrate Communion in Eastern rite Catholic churches, but not in churches that are not united with Rome. Communion of the Orthodox Church is recognized as valid, but a Catholic may celebrate Communion of the Orthodox Church only in exceptional cases. This applies when no Roman rite is available or when a person is in danger of death (Canon #844).

Part III

The Sacraments of Healing and Forgiveness:
PENANCE AND ANOINTING OF THE SICK

Because our human nature yearns for wholeness, we search for ways to cope with our weaknesses and frailties. Realizing that God, too, desires our wholeness, the Church provides healing grace and rejuvenation for body and soul through the sacraments of penance and anointing of the sick.

PENANCE

"You are forgiven" are comforting words in any language. To reach out in love and forget injury is a Godlike quality. In fact, this is precisely the way the Lord deals with us. Most especially this compassion and love of Christ is experienced in the sacrament of forgiveness.

Over the years, this sacrament has been known by various names. It was called penance to signify the need to atone for sins. It was called confession to underscore the penitent's telling of sins. Because Vatican II stresses God's forgiveness and healing, today it is often referred to as the sacrament of reconciliation. Here, we will refer to the sacrament of penance and the rite of reconciliation.

Penance Continues Jesus' Mission

The theme of forgiveness pervaded Jesus' ministry. After the Resurrection, Jesus clearly enunciated his compassionate forgiveness: "Peace be with you. As the Father has sent me, so I send you. If you forgive the sins of any, they are forgiven them" (John 20:21, 23). With this as their principle, early Christians committed their lives wholly to Christ. Once baptized they were totally converted and many were martyred for their convictions.

Ordinary foibles of human nature were forgiven through Eucharist, fraternal correction, and in community gatherings. After the persecutions, those guilty of grave sin or scandal were readmitted into the Christian community following a period of public canonical penance. Because this austerity was not popular, many sinners postponed a return to the Church until they were near death.

In actuality, few Christians had need of public penance. But because all people are subject to human shortcomings, the Church in the fourth century prescribed a special time of penance: the forty days before Easter known as Lent.

In the sixth century, however, Irish monks preached on the mainland and initiated private confession as a means of spiritual guidance. This devotion became quite popular and soon spread throughout Europe. When the Church recognized its spiritual benefits, confession became the accepted form of sacramental forgiveness. At the Second Council of Lyons (1274), this sacrament was numbered among the seven sacraments, and confession was prescribed at least once a year for those guilty of serious sin.

6th c
confession =
spiritual
guidance

During the Middle Ages, theologians spent a great deal of energy discussing moral questions and issues concerning mortal and venial sin, perfect and imperfect contrition, and the satisfaction due to sin. During that time, the doctrines of purgatory and indulgences were developed.

By the time the Council of Trent convened, confession was standardized and the priest was seen as a judge with divine power to absolve. Booklets stipulated which penances were to be given. The sacrament of penance (confession) became primarily a "telling" of sins. To forestall abuses and preserve anonymity, enclosed cubicles called confessionals became part of every Catholic church.

Penance After Vatican II: This procedure lasted until Vatican II, when the focus of the sacrament was placed on the healing forgiveness of Christ, which is the essential aspect of the sacrament. This deeper understanding of the nature of the sacrament has led to other insights which affect the rite of reconciliation.

Penance Celebrates the Presence of Jesus in Symbolic Ritual

The symbols and ritual of the sacrament of penance are tied to the spirit of Vatican II. Many of the old and long-standing mind-sets and routines were examined in the process of refashioning the celebration of Jesus' presence in the forgiveness of sins.

The Symbols and Rite of Reconciliation: The changes of Vatican II regarding the sacrament of penance focus on our attitude toward sin and forgiveness rather than on striking external changes. But how we think about penance does affect how we approach the sacrament. Here we list some of the chief shifts of emphasis of the new rite of reconciliation.

- God is more interested in forgiving us than in listening to a "grocery list" of our shortcomings.

- God is love and desires us to be at peace. As humans, we all sin, but there's always the divine plea to conversion. "Come back to me" beckons us to Christ's healing forgiveness.

- Sin breaks down the goodness in the world. The "domino effect" of our failures increase evil if we do not reform our sinful ways. The opportunity of "beginning again" with a clean slate and peace of heart is ours through the sacrament of penance.

The renewed rite allows for three ways in which penance can be celebrated: individual confession, communal penance, and general absolution.

Individual Confession: A prayerful reflection, the examination of conscience, prepares us for individual confession. We need not dwell on specific acts ("What sins did I commit?"), but ought rather to consider the subtle attitudes that underlie all sins : "In what area do I need God's healing?" To assist in recalling our failings, some prefer to use a standard form based on the Eight Beatitudes or the Ten Commandments. We can then choose to celebrate penance in the traditional confessional or face to face.

Individual, private confession is a renewing experience. The priest greets the penitent, Scripture is read, and the penitent confesses his or her sins. The penitent then prays an Act of Contrition after the priest gives him or her a penance. The priest then offers absolution, and the celebration concludes with a proclamation of praise.

Communal Penance: The celebration of reconciliation in a community setting combines public prayer and individual confession, witnessing that we are a reconciling assembly. At the communal penance service, the community gathers in prayer and reflection before and after individual confession. This is a meaningful sacramental service celebrated especially during Lent, Advent, and retreats.

General Absolution: When individual confession is impossible due to a shortage of priests or other reasons, general absolution is allowed, but its use is restricted to extraordinary, urgent situations.

Penance Connects Our Faith to Our Life Situations

The sacramental rite is a part of the natural rhythm of life. We never reach the point of "having it made." Our call to conversion of heart is an ongoing, never-to-be-completed process.

The sacramental graces of penance are truly effective when we live in the spirit of forgiveness as we pray in the Our Father, "forgive us as we forgive." Reconciliation needs to pervade every aspect of our life as we strive to bring peace and harmony in our encounters and relationships.

Penance and the Individual: Psychology today propounds what the Church has long known: confession is good for the soul. When we externalize and express our deepest feelings of guilt, we feel a sense of relief and can carry on with greater ease. The rise of myriad support groups attests to the satisfaction derived from unburdening oneself. In the sacrament of penance, we have at our disposal an effective means to bring about our inner harmony with God, the world, and ourselves.

Penance and the Church Community: Today, we are more aware of our global interdependence. The world is as good and wicked as are those who live in it. In every culture, sin and sinful attitudes diminish goodness and intensify evil. As members of the Church, we build up or tear down the Body of Christ in the world. Our personal sins affect all of society.

This communal aspect of sin is vital to our understanding of the consequences of our actions and is the focal point of our celebration of reconciliation.

Pastoral Concerns: Perhaps the most pressing pastoral concern regarding the sacrament of penance is that many people find confessing to a priest very difficult. People wonder why they cannot just confess their sins to God. They overlook the fact that sin is not a private affair.

The healing power of Christ is made visible through Christ's official representative, the ordained priest. Sin offends against the community, and so the priest represents and forgives in the name of the community.

That Catholics are not making regular use of the sacrament of penance is another pastoral concern. This attitude stems from our culture's loss of a sense of sin. Immorality is condoned and even glorified, as portrayed in the media. As a result, moral apathy has greatly diminished the painful reality of sin. We need a renewal of values that sensitizes us to right and wrong, and a deeper appreciation of God's compassionate forgiveness in the sacrament of penance.

Age, sickness, and death are inevitable parts of the cycle of life. Time does not destroy the human person, but prepares us for life eternal. The Church, in her pastoral care and in continuing Jesus' healing ministry, brings comfort in times of physical distress through the sacrament of anointing of the sick.

ANOINTING OF THE SICK

Anointing of the Sick Continues Jesus' Mission

From earliest days, people sought aid for the ravages of sickness and age using herbs, oils, chants, and spells for healing. Much of Jesus' ministry was spent healing the sick. The miracles of Jesus in the New Testament testify to cures. Jesus also commissioned the apostles to heal. (See Mark 6:7.) The Acts of the Apostles records that people brought the sick to Peter and John; the mere shadows of these powerful healers could bring health to the infirmed.

The Epistle of James gave explicit directions about ministry to the sick: "Are any among you sick? They should call for the elders of the church and have them pray over them, anointing them with oil" (James 5:14).

This practice continued in the early Church; the healing power of the Lord continued through prayers and simple anointings. Laypersons, too, took blessed oil from church into homes and prayed with and anointed the sick.

Gradually this healing rite developed into an elaborate church ceremony performed exclusively by clergy. Because it mirrored the healing actions of Jesus, this ritual was named a sacrament at the Second Council of Lyons.

In the Middle Ages, healing methods were so severe, such as bloodletting, amputations, and hot irons, that medical aid was sought only at the point of death. Sacramental healing was also sought only at the point of death. This anointing was the sacrament of the dying, or the last rites. The Communion received became known as *viaticum*, which is Latin for "going with you on the way." In many places, the final anointing was an elaborate ceremony. The dying were brought into the church and many priests laid hands on them and anointed them. Later this practice was abandoned; the sick were anointed privately. In 1545, the Council of Trent affirmed the sacrament of extreme unction, or the last anointing, as one of the seven sacraments.

Anointing of the Sick After Vatican II: To recapture the authentic meaningfulness for the sacrament as Christ's healing for the sick, Vatican II changed the name from extreme unction to sacrament of the sick, or anointing of the sick.

The revised ritual for anointing of the sick includes pastoral care of the sick, which focuses on the Church's overall ministry to the sick. Hospitals and parishes offer pastoral care services that support the sick and the dying and their families. Clinical Pastoral Education (CPE) courses are often required for health care personnel and pastoral ministers.

Anointing of the Sick Celebrates the Presence of Jesus in Symbolic Ritual

In coping with illness and disease, persons have discovered ways to alleviate the pangs of pain and bring healing. This is nothing new; it's as old as humankind itself.

The Symbols and Rite of Anointing of the Sick: Oil has always been a universal anodyne, and so it is the appropriate matter for the sacrament of the sick. Olive oil is recommended, but any plant oil that has been blessed can be used for the sacramental anointing.

The gesture of touch also has deep meaning in anointing of the sick. Just as Jesus used touch and bodily contact in his healings, so also the healing touch of the priest and of those present provide peace and assurance at a time when one feels most alone.

Those who are sick, the aged, the infirmed, those preparing for surgery, and children who can grasp the meaning of the sacrament can celebrate anointing of the sick. A person may celebrate the sacrament whenever his or her condition worsens.

Because the sacrament of anointing of the sick is for those who are sick, ideally it should be administered when one is able to respond prayerfully. The Church prays not only *for* the sick but *with* the sick as well. Along with the community, the sick person intercedes with the Lord to be healed. Therefore, anointing should not be put off until one can no longer participate fully in the prayers; proper preparation demands that one be aware of celebrating the sacrament. Anointing is not a private, secret ritual but a celebration of the Lord's healing.

Ordinarily, one person is anointed. Occasionally, a communal anointing of the sick is celebrated as a healing service or with a liturgy in church or in a healthcare facility.

Anointing of the sick is administered by a priest who, allowing for flexibility in each case, selects the readings and prayers accordingly. If the person celebrating the sacrament is at the point of death, the ritual prayers are said for the dying. If the patient has died, the sacrament is not administered, but the priest can pray and bless the body for the comfort of the bereaved.

The priest anoints the forehead and the open palms of the hands or other parts appropriate to the case. Only the forehead is anointed in an emergency.

Anointing of the Sick Connects Our Faith to Our Life Situation

We all are called to be healers and to bring consolation to others. The sacrament of anointing of the sick helps us remember the redemptive quality of suffering.

Anointing of the Sick and the Individual: When we celebrate the sacrament of anointing, we profess our faith in the healing power of Christ; we witness to the sufferings of Christ. Our feelings of limitation and fragility help us discover the freedom in letting go of natural life in exchange for a life of eternal happiness.

Anointing of the sick not only brings spiritual peace but also brings forgiveness of sins and the punishment due to them. If we cannot go to confession, our sins are remitted.

Anointing of the Sick and the Church Community: The person in pain needs the blessing and support of the entire faith community because we all are reminded of the fragile state of our human body. As members of the Church, we need to be concerned about and responsible for alleviating pain and suffering. It alerts us that our caring must extend beyond the sick room to the other social ills and injustices rampant in society today.

The anointing by the priest represents the healing power of the Lord being poured out into the whole Church. Although it is one person who ordinarily celebrates the sacrament, the prayers of the whole Church provide comfort and support. Those present at an anointing witness the healing power of the Church and are afforded an opportunity to reflect on the spiritual dimensions of sickness.

Pastoral Concerns: People today are becoming more accustomed to the fact that the sacrament of anointing of the sick is not for the dying alone. If the attitude still exists, we should not wait until one is at the point of death to call a priest.

However, we must remember the basic purpose of the anointing of the sick as a sacramental healing grace for the seriously ill, the infirm, and the aged. The sacrament is not meant to be a devotional practice for those who feel a need for healing.

The Church acknowledges that there are other valid ways to heal and that certain persons possess the gift of healing. A service over which a faith healer presides is ordinarily a paraliturgical healing service, unless it is designated as a sacrament. These services are beneficial and sometimes effect cures. However, there must be a clear distinction between a paraliturgical healing service, which can be grace-filled, and the sacrament of anointing of the sick, the official Church sacrament.

Part IV

The Sacraments of Commitment and Service:
HOLY ORDERS AND MATRIMONY

L ife commitments are investments and divestments, involving both self-sacrifice and service to others. As the pig told the hen when they chanced upon a billboard of ham and eggs, "For you, it's only involvement; but for me, it's total commitment."

Since married life and priesthood are significant life decisions that demand wholehearted commitment, the Church celebrates and blesses these vocations with the sacramental graces of holy orders and matrimomy.

HOLY ORDERS

The priestly mission of Christ continues in those ordained and empowered through the sacrament of orders which is composed of three degrees, each having specific roles.

At the first level of orders, one is ordained as a transitional deacon in preparation for the priesthood, or as a permanent deacon for the ministry of service. The second level of orders is the priesthood, which empowers a transitional deacon to celebrate Mass and the sacraments. Bishops are ordained with the fullness of orders, the third level, which endows them with ecclesial and administrative authority.

DEACON, PRIESTHOOD, and BISHOP

Holy Orders Continues Jesus' Mission

The Acts of the Apostles records the common lifestyle of the early Christian communities. Each person built up the Body of Christ in various ministries. For the first two centuries after Jesus' death, there was no priest in charge because priesthood, as we know it today, did not exist. The Church was loosely structured, bound together by the community of believers who followed "the Way." Those who presided at worship and prayer assemblies were usually men who had natural leadership abilities. They came to be known as *episcopoi* (bishops) and were assisted by "presbyters" (elders) and deacons.

When Christianity became the official religion of the Empire in A.D. 381, a more stable hierarchy emerged with the bishop as the leader of the community; all ministries flowed from his authority. The bishop commissioned presbyters, through the laying on of hands, to assist him in ministering to communities of faith in outlying districts.

After the fall of the Roman Empire in the fifth century, barbarian tribes converted to Christianity. To assist in the task of evangelization, monks who had lived in monasteries and the desert were summoned. Thus a new form of minister emerged: one totally committed to spiritual things through a celibate lifestyle. Seen as an asset to ministry, celibacy became an accepted and preferred lifestyle for clergy, but it was not mandatory.

By the twelfth century the sacramental system was determined; orders was named one of the seven sacraments and celibacy became a Church law. Since priests often came from the nobility, the official clerical hierarchy emerged as a class distinct from the laity, having its own privileges and powers.

The Reformation (1517) spoke out against the abuses of powers and prestige that were rampant at the time. The Council of Trent affirmed the power and authority of the priest as dispenser of sacramental graces. Priests were to receive training and formation in special schools called seminaries, especially regarding the proper rubrics for the sacraments and the Mass.

Holy Orders Since Vatican II: The deeper insights of Vatican II concerning the essential nature of the Church greatly affected our understanding of priesthood. The Church is the people of God and all persons are called to universal holiness. Although this new insight has not completely obliterated the distinction between clergy and laity, Vatican II called for greater lay participation in the active ministry of the Church.

The renewal of priestly life emphasizes the priesthood as a consecration for service rather than power. Vatican II also reinstated the permanent diaconate as a ministry in its own right.

Holy Orders Celebrates the Presence of Jesus in Symbolic Ritual

One who aspires to become a priest must be motivated by the overriding desire to serve Christ by serving others.

The Symbols and Rite of Holy Orders: The ordination Mass is a powerful expression of the Church's mission, symbolizing new life for the Church through the newly ordained.

The ordinations of deacons, priests, and bishops most often take place on separate occasions. The rite of ordination is administered by the bishop at a special liturgy usually celebrated in the cathedral, the main church of a diocese. Because the rites for deacon, priest, and bishop are similar, with appropriate adaptations, we here consider the rite of ordination of a priest.

The men to be ordained are presented to the bishop and affirm that they are willing and ready to commit themselves to the ministry of the priesthood. The candidates are then affirmed by the congregation, with applause or some apt sign of approval.

After the homily, the bishop again asks the candidates if they are aware of their serious decision. Each one affirms his willingness to live the priestly life and pledges obedience to the bishop. The candidates lie prostrate on the floor, while the Litany of the Saints is prayed.

The essential part of the rite occurs when the bishop lays his hands on each candidate's head. This is an ancient symbol of being invested with priestly powers. Other priests in attendance also lay hands on the newly ordained, and a prayer of consecration is prayed by the bishop.

The new priests are then vested with the stole and chasuble as symbols of their priesthood. Their hands are anointed by the bishop, and they accept the vessels and elements used at Mass. After a sign of peace is exchanged, they join with the bishop and other priests in concelebrating their first Mass.

There is a distinction between diocesan priests and religious priests. A diocesan priest is under the aegis of his bishop and commissioned to serve in a specific diocese. A religious priest belongs to a religious or missionary community, such as the Redemptorists or the Jesuits, and is under his religious superior and the bishop in whose diocese he serves. A monk belongs to a contemplative community, such as the Trappists, and can be ordained a priest or profess religious vows as a Brother. Contemplatives devote their time to prayer and some work which supports them.

The Permanent Deacon: After centuries of being a preliminary step to the priesthood, the permanent diaconate was reinstated in 1967 as a distinct ministry. A permanent deacon can be a married or celibate man, at least thirty-five years of age, with a secular occupation. After a period of spiritual formation, he celebrates the first level of orders and is appointed by the bishop to a specific ministry.

The permanent deacon can preach homilies, distribute Communion, preside at baptisms and prayer services, be the ecclesial witness at a wedding, assist at liturgical functions, and administer sacramentals. Deacons are an asset in the Church due to increased priest shortages and a call for lay leadership. Permanent deacons also serve well as marriage counselors and are distinct witnesses representing the Church in the work place.

Holy Orders Connects Our Faith to Our Life Situations

In his liturgical role, the ordained priest makes it possible for the sacramental life of the Church to continue. Vatican II has also recognized the "priesthood of all believers," the "priestly role" of all those who participate in the mission of Christ in virtue of baptism.

Holy Orders and the Individual: Every priestly vocation is a mystery of grace, a divine gift that requires serious discernment and a free response. After years of theological studies and pastoral experience, having been judged capable of living the priestly life, one is called to ordination. Because a priest is Christ's official representative, he needs to develop a personal, intimate, spiritual relationship with Christ. First and foremost, the priest is ordained for the service of mediating and presiding at liturgical and sacramental functions.

But his role is changing and more demanding in our fast-moving world. The priest today is also expected to be counselor, group dynamics expert, upholder of social justice, caregiver, organizer, theologian, and implementer of Vatican II. But no matter how many hats he wears, the priest, through his witness and countercultural, celibate lifestyle, points to the spiritual dimension of life. He is, above all, a cogent symbol of Christ's abiding presence.

Holy Orders and the Church Community: Every ordination brings growth to the Church. The renewed rite of ordination stresses primarily the community-related aspect of the sacrament, service for others being its primary objective. No matter what a priest does, he does so for the community. The priest is the standard-bearer of the faith community; he directs, guides, builds up, and provides leadership for the spiritual welfare of the community.

The renewal of Vatican II has greatly affected the relationship of the priest to the community of faith. Today, we speak of partnership, mutuality, shared responsibility, and interdependence between priest and people. This new climate and style of leadership allow for a more vibrant Church as priest and laity work together to build up the Body of Christ. The priest remains a cogent reminder of God's abiding presence and concern for his people.

Each ordination summons all Catholics to their personal role in carrying out Christ's mission. We all can share according to our circumstances in some work of the Church. Whether it is in specific ministries connected with the Church or in our ordinary daily work, we all are witnesses to Christ and are called to be Christ for others.

Each ordination calls us to reflect on the gift of the priesthood which provides service and leadership in our communities of faith. We need to respectfully support those called to serve in the priesthood and pray that others will follow the call.

Pastoral Concerns: The law of celibacy is perhaps one of the major pastoral concerns of the sacraments of orders. Celibacy is being challenged today more than ever before. While celibacy is not essential to the priesthood, it remains the norm for priests of the Roman rite. The Church looks upon celibacy as a special gift of the Lord and is committed to upholding it. By not attaching oneself to any particular person, the celibate priest is a powerful reminder that all human relationships have their source and root in God.

Perhaps the most widely felt pastoral concern in the Church today regarding orders is the shortage of priestly vocations. Although there is increased participation of laity in the ministries of the Church, the priest makes it possible for the liturgical and sacramental life of the Church to continue. The dearth of priests has somewhat been eased by the admission of second-career men to the priesthood and policies concerning a more equable distribution of priests to areas that have a shortage of priests.

Although optional celibacy and women's ordination are debated issues, the Church is determined not to depart from its long-standing law and deepset tradition of a celibate male priesthood.

MATRIMONY

Every culture considers marriage a most special event and celebrates it with elaborate rituals. The Bible records that marriage was in the plan of God from the dawn of creation. The Church recognizes this divine design; throughout her history, she has upheld the sacredness of marriage and, through the sacramental graces of matrimony, has assisted couples to live out the challenges that married life entails.

Matrimony Continues Jesus' Mission

God's plan for man and woman to share life and procreate is graphically described in the opening chapters of Genesis. The people of Israel heeded God's command and worked out an elaborate system of laws governing marriage.

Jesus reinforced God's design and recognized marriage as a special lasting relationship. Having lived most of his earthly life within the embrace of a loving family and household, Jesus believed in celebrating life's important events as seen in his attendance and first miracle at the wedding in Cana. We have no indication that Jesus specifically instituted marriage as a sacrament, but his attitude toward the union of man and woman as an indissoluble bond has been a Catholic tenet of faith from the earliest days of the Church: "What God has joined together, let no one separate" (Matthew 19:6). Saint Paul regarded marriage as sacred, and in the Epistle to the Ephesians, he compared the marital union to the relationship of Jesus with the Church.

The early Christians upheld marriage as a sacred bond, but according to the customs of the time, marriage was a private family affair often arranged by the parents and regulated by civil authority. Later, some Church Fathers, especially Saint Augustine, taught that sex was the animal instinct in humans and that marriage was necessary only for the continuation of the human race. This notion dominated Church teaching and affected the theology of marriage for centuries.

Only gradually did the Church become directly involved in presiding at marriages. Clergy who were wedding guests were often asked to bless the couple after they were wed by the civil authority. Later this blessing took place at the door of the church. By the eleventh century, to prevent abuses of forced consent, the wedding ceremony began to take place in church and was presided over by the clergy with special nuptial blessings and prayers.

In support of the sacredness and indissolubility of the marriage bond, the Church, at the Second Council of Lyons, numbered marriage as one of the seven sacraments. Because the primary goal of marriage was the begetting of children, the sacrament was named *matrimony*, from the root word for *mother*.

The Council of Trent (1545-1563) set down stringent marriage laws. The sacrament of matrimony was defined as a legal contract valid only if it took place in the presence of a priest and two witnesses, with procreation concerning marriage (111 canons). To safeguard the sacredness of marriage, the Church has dramatically shifted its understanding of marriage to a deeper level.

In reinterpreting God's plan of redemption, Vatican II emphasizes marriage as a covenant relationship, like the relationship of Christ to the Church. Vatican II explains the marital union in scriptural terms as an "intimate partnership of life and love" (*Pastoral Constitution on the Church in the Modern World*, #48). Greater stress is now laid upon the couple's self-giving to each other as a way to grow in God's love and be a more viable sign of Christ.

Matrimony Celebrates the Presence of Jesus in Symbolic Ritual

Since our society does not seriously respect the stability of marriage, and since we are surrounded by popular cultural values, it is most important to provide adequate marriage preparation for couples. This helps ascertain the compatibility of the parties and their psychological readiness for the challenges of the married state. Thorough preparation also helps the couple fully understand the symbolism and rituals used to celebrate their life of commitment.

The Rite and Symbols of Matrimony: To become validly married in the eyes of the Church, one is required to be of a mature age and free to marry; one must also freely choose to marry and must not be closely related by blood to the other party. Likewise, one must be physically capable of the marriage act and open to the possibility of new life.

Because sacramental marriage is a sign of Christ's abiding love, it is solemnly celebrated in a special rite—ideally during a special liturgy called a nuptial Mass. The couple is encouraged to assist in planning the ceremony and the liturgy regarding the music, prayers, and Scripture passages. This option allows for a more meaningful celebration and makes the ceremony more personal for the couple.

The revised rite of marriage portrays marriage as a covenant relationship. It is a simple rite, the key element being the mutual and free consent which the couple publicly expresses to each other in the presence of the gathered community. The mutual affection of the couple for each other, expressed in the solemn exchange of the marriage vows, is the heart of the sacramental celebration.

Unlike other sacraments that are administered by a priest, the couple administers the sacrament to each other. The priest or deacon serves as the official ecclesial witness and the wedding attendants act as witnesses of the community. The ceremony is an outward expression of worship and faith.

The supplementary ceremonies surrounding the couple's exchange of vows provide meaningful symbolism and add to the solemnity of the occasion. The exchange of rings represents the total exclusive partnership the couple pledges to each other. Another optional tradition, a nuptial candle lit from the couple's individual candles, symbolizes the unity of life and love they vow to share.

The rite of matrimony concludes with an official blessing; the whole Church joins in prayer for the couple's happiness and God's abiding help for their uncertain future.

No matter how simple or elaborate the ceremony, the wedding rite celebrates the joyous start of a mutual effort toward growth and maturity in a loving, lasting relationship.

Matrimony Connects Our Faith to Our Life Situations

The harmony and love of a happily married couple stands as a cogent sign of the harmony of all human relationships. Matrimony's sign of unity challenges all persons to strive for meaningful relationships in life. To "increase and multiply" may apply primarily to marriage, but the Genesis mandate extends beyond the marital bond; all humans are called to live fully and to bring forth goodness in the world. The sacramentality of marriage is experienced when persons share their giftedness and caring as do the spouses in a true marriage relationship.

Matrimony and the Individual: When a man and woman enter into the permanent relationship of love in marriage, they portray the love that God has shown in creation. Moreover, their self-giving love for each other mirrors the bond of unity that Christ has for the Church.

Individuals who enter the married state enter a new way of life in which all things are shared. The couple becomes key agents of helping each other grow as persons and in holiness. The couple, being mutually responsible for each other, does so through a fidelity which is lasting and exclusive.

Matrimony and the Church Community: The couple's pledge of love to each other is a vibrant sign of the Lord's continuing mission among the people of God, celebrated in the presence of the community who lovingly affirm the couple. The newlyweds form another miniature community of faith. Their family unit is a "domestic church," the arena in which God is experienced through family intimacy and spiritual values are nurtured.

Marriage contributes to the growth of the Christian community, which is as strong as its families, the basis of society. The stronger and more solid the human relationships and bonds of love within the family unit, so much more is the Christian community a witness to Christ's love and presence.

Pastoral Concerns: There are a number of pastoral problems relating to marriage that the Church is aware of and attempts to meet with compassion and understanding.

- **Annulments:** The Church upholds the indissolubility of the marriage bond and does not condone divorce. Yet, the Church recognizes that some relationships lack certain essential elements vital to a sacramental marriage: freedom, maturity, responsible decision. The Church also realizes the complications and harm that many innocent people often endure; in response, she is understanding and compassionate and may grant an annulment. This decree of nullity is granted only if, in the eyes of the Church, there has not been a valid marriage. This annulment is the official statement by the Church that, after thorough investigation, no sacramental marriage ever existed. When a decree of nullity is officially granted, the couple is free to remarry.

- **Interfaith and inter-racial marriages:** Although couples who share the same faith and culture have a distinct advantage over those who do not, interfaith and inter-racial marriages are on the rise. The Church recognizes interfaith and inter-racial marriages provided the ceremonies take place in a Catholic church, or in the place of worship of the party who is not Catholic, and provided a Catholic priest or deacon is present as the Church's witness.

  Interfaith marriages face the issues of raising their children in the Catholic tradition. The Church

asks that Catholic spouses promise to do everything possible to raise the children in the faith. Non-Catholic spouses are no longer required to make any promise at all about raising the children Catholic. But they must be informed of the promise made by the Catholic party. The church's main concern is that family unity, love, and religious values are upheld.

- *Divorce and separation:* The Church recognizes the many Catholics affected by divorce. One of the growing and much needed services the Church can offer today is ministry to the divorced and separated. Persons suffering the pain of loss and the fear of an uncertain future as a result of divorce can find support and healing through sharing with others. Parishes need to consider this compassionate outreach to the divorced and separated as a vital and necessary pastoral concern.

CONCLUSION

Jesus' coming into the world was not meant for only the few thousand people in Palestine whose lives he touched. Rather, his presence transcends space and time and extends into our age through the Church and the sacraments.

Jesus continues to invite, heal, nourish, forgive, strengthen, provide spiritual leaders, and bless life commitments. Through the sacraments, the promise of Jesus is most perfectly fulfilled: "I am with you always" (Matthew 28:20).

ABOUT THE AUTHOR

Sister Charlene Altemose, MSC, is a Missionary sister of the Most Sacred Heart (Reading, Pennsylvania) with degrees in education, theology, and journalism. Her ministries have included teaching college theology, writing newspaper columns and articles, directing parish adult education, and being active in interfaith activities and the Council of Churches.

Sister Charlene was awarded a Fulbright scholarship to India and a Christian Leadership grant to Israel. As a result of her scholarship excellence, she was invited to be a presenter at the 1993 Council for a Parliament of World Religions.

Author of *Why Do Catholics...?* (Brown-Roa), and *What You Should Know About the Mass* and *What You Should Know About the Catechism of the Catholic Church* (Liguori), Sister Charlene also gives workshops, retreats, and in-service or adult education programs.

More books by Sister Charlene Altemose

What You Should Know About the Mass

Charlene Altemose, MSC

Explains the role played by those present and the symbolic gestures used in the Mass, outlines the liturgical seasons, and details each section of the Mass. $2.95

Also available in Spanish
Lo Que Usted Debe Saber Sobre la Misa $2.95

What You Should Know About the Catechism of the Catholic Church

Charlene Altemose, MSC

Historical background to the new *Catechism*, its rationale and purpose. Address-es the individual's response in faith and practical use of the *Catechism* in classroom study, personal study, adult initiation, group discussion, and more. $1.95

Also available in Spanish
Lo Que Usted Debe Saber Sobre el Catecismo de la Iglesia Catolica $1.95

Also from Liguori

The Privilege of Being Catholic
Oscar Lukefahr, C.M.

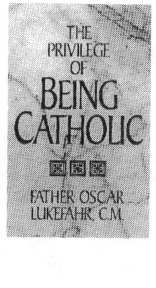

Using Scripture, history, and revelation, Father Lukefahr highlights the tenets of faith that form the heart of Catholic tradition. Explores how the Catholic sacramental view of the world is expressed in every aspect of Catholic life. $7.95

Also
The Privilege of Being Catholic
Workbook $2.95

Order from your local bookstore or write to

Liguori Publications
Box 060
Liguori, MO 63057-9999

Please add 15% to your total for postage and handling ($3.50 minimum, $15 maximum).